Collins

Phonics Success

Louis Fidge and Christine Moorcroft

Contents

Contents

Introduction

What is phonics?
Phonics is the relationship between sounds (phonemes) and letters or groups of letters (graphemes). Learning phonics involves listening to sounds, recognising sounds and discriminating between sounds as well as learning how sounds are represented by letters.

Phonics Practice Activities 2 is based on current practice in schools and presents letters and sounds in ways that should be familiar to the learners from their school work. This book will help the learners to learn to read and spell and to improve their reading and spelling using phonics.

Phonics for children (ages 5 to 6)
Literacy includes reading and writing, and phonics is important in both of these areas. This book builds on the learner's previous learning (see *Phonics Practice Activities 1*). It introduces a number of new sounds, and the letters that can represent the sounds, including different ways of spelling sounds they have already learned.

In addition to learning phonics, learners should have opportunities to:
- read and enjoy stories, poems, rhymes and jingles
- read non-fiction texts, including signs, labels, captions, notes and so on.

This book helps learners to learn the relationship between sounds and letters. They will learn:
- alphabetical order and the use of upper- and lower-case letters
- vowel sounds that are spelled using more than one letter
- different ways of spelling the same sounds
- different sounds represented by the same letters
- unusual spellings of vowel sounds, for example: 'or' for the 'ur' sound in words like 'worm', 'word' and 'work'
- unusual spellings of consonant sounds, for example: 'ph' for the 'f' sound; 'silent' letters, such as 'k' in 'knee', 'b' in 'comb', 't' in 'listen'.

How this book is organised
Letters of the alphabet (p. 6–11) further develops the learner's understanding of upper- and lower-case letters, and alphabetical order.

Vowel digraphs introduces vowel sounds spelled with two letters: ay, ou, oy, ir, ea, aw, ew, oe, au, ie, ey for the 'ay' sound, and ey for the 'ee' sound.

Split digraphs features words with long vowel sounds (such as the 'i' in 'kite') that are spelled with two letters separated by a consonant (e.g. i–e in 'kite', a–e in bake).

Alternative vowel pronunciations introduces different ways of pronouncing vowels that have already been introduced. For example, the letter 'i' has been introduced for the 'i' sound in 'tip', 'bit' and so on, but it can also be pronounced in the same way as 'igh' in 'high' in words such as 'tiny', 'Ipod', 'mild'.

Alternative spellings for vowel sounds introduces different ways of spelling vowel sounds such as the 'or' sound in 'for'. This sound can also be spelled 'ore', 'oor' or 'our'.

Alternative spellings for consonant phonemes introduces different and more unusual ways of spelling the consonant sounds 'w' (wh), 'f' (ph), 'ch' (tch and tu) and 'j' (dge).

Alternative consonant pronunciations introduces less common ways of pronouncing consonants 'ch' (as 'k' in Christmas and as 'sh' in chef). Other unusual consonants introduced are 'ci' and 'ti' tor 'sh' (as in 'special' and 'mention'), 's' for 'z' (as in 'please'), other 'c' and 'g' sounds and the 'zh' sound represented by 's' in words such as 'treasure'.

Silent letters features 'g', 'k', 'w', 'b' and 't' in words such as 'gnaw', 'knee', 'dumb' and 'listen'.

What have I learned?
This section provides activities to help the learner assess what has been learned. It helps to determine what further practice the learner needs.

Animal alphabet

Letters a–m

Say the name of each animal.
Write the letters for the first sound.
Write the first letter in the box.

a 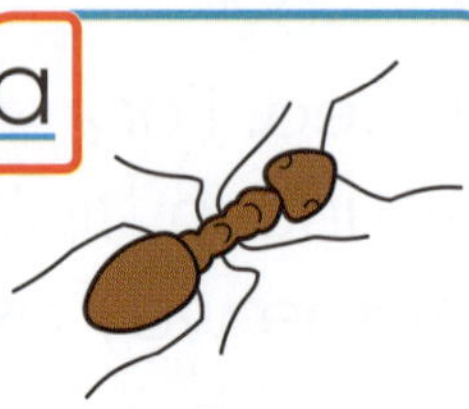 ant

_ 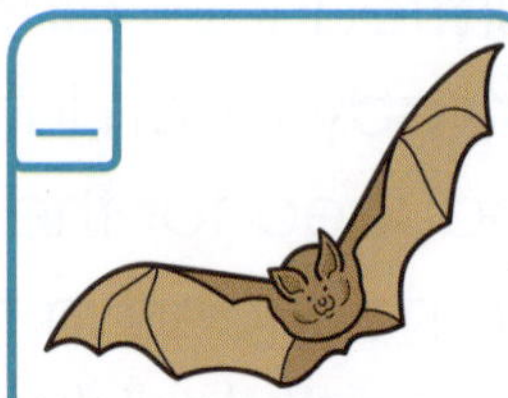 _at

_  _at

_  _og

_  _lephant

_  _rog

_  _oat

_  _orse

_  _guana

_  _aguar

_  _angaroo

_  _ion

_  _ouse

Teacher's tip

Ask the learner to name the animal in each picture. Give help where necessary (especially for the more unusual animals, such as iguana). Then ask him/her to name the animal in the first picture. Ask the learner to say the sound the word begins with and then to name the letter and write it in the box.

Letters n-z

Say the name of each animal.

Write the letters for the first sound.

Write the first letter in the box.

n

newt

_strich

_anda

_uail

_abbit

_nake

_ortoise

_mbrella bird

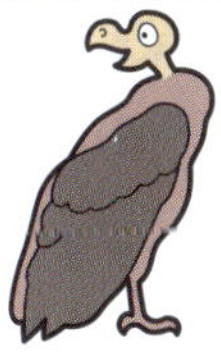

_ulture

_olf

_-ray fish

_ak

_ebra

Teacher's tip

Ask the learner to name the animal in each picture. Give help where necessary (especially for the more unusual animals, such as vulture). Ask the learner to say the sound the word begins with and then to name the letter and write it in the box. N.B. quail begins with the sound spelled qu although the first letter is q so the learner should write qu.

Alphabetical order

Rocket alphabet

Take the rocket to each star in order.

Dot-to-dot alphabet

Join up the dots in alphabetical order to make a picture.

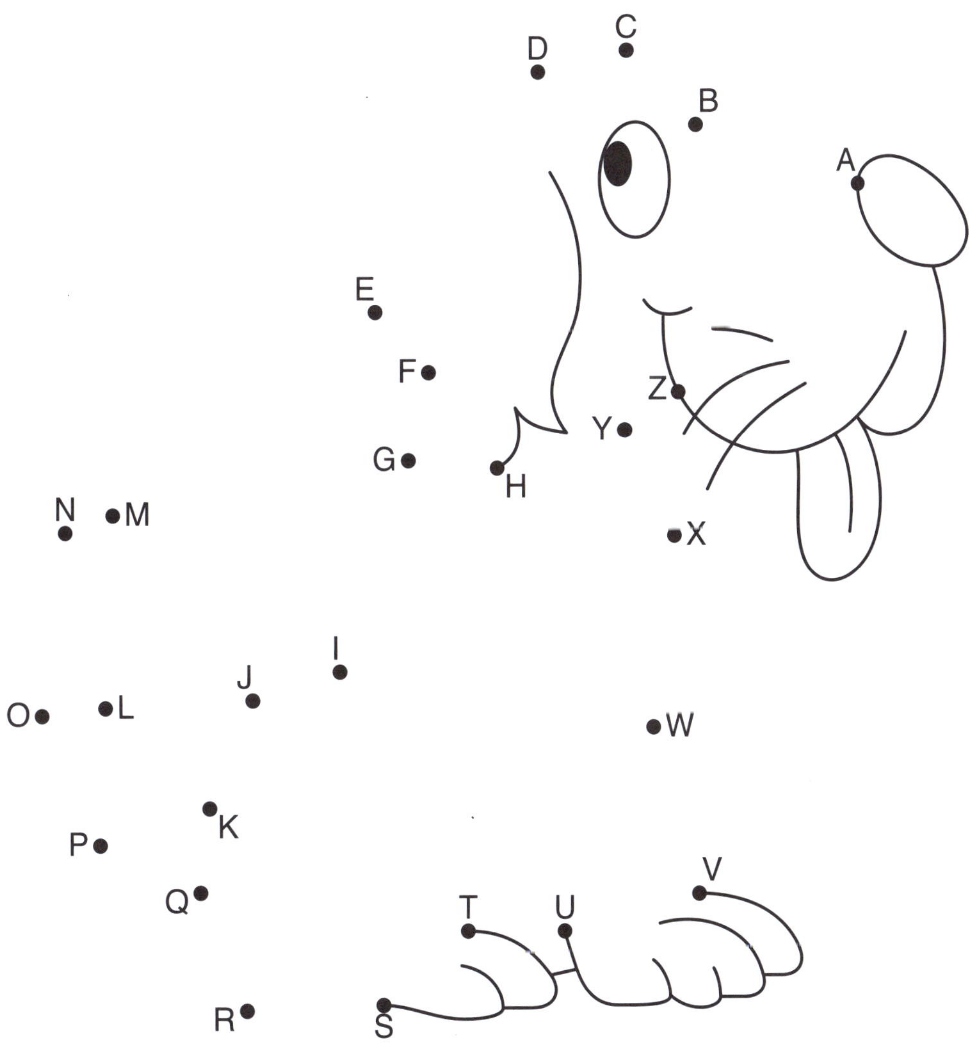

Teacher's tip	Ask the learner to find the first letter of the alphabet and say its name. Ask 'What comes next?' Ask questions such as: 'Which letter comes after h?', 'What comes after t?' and so on. After the learner has completed the page ask: 'Which letter comes before b?', What comes before h?' and so on.

Upper- and lower-case letters

Aa Bb Cc Dd

Ee Ff Gg

Hh Ii Jj Kk

Ll Mm

Upper- and lower-case letters

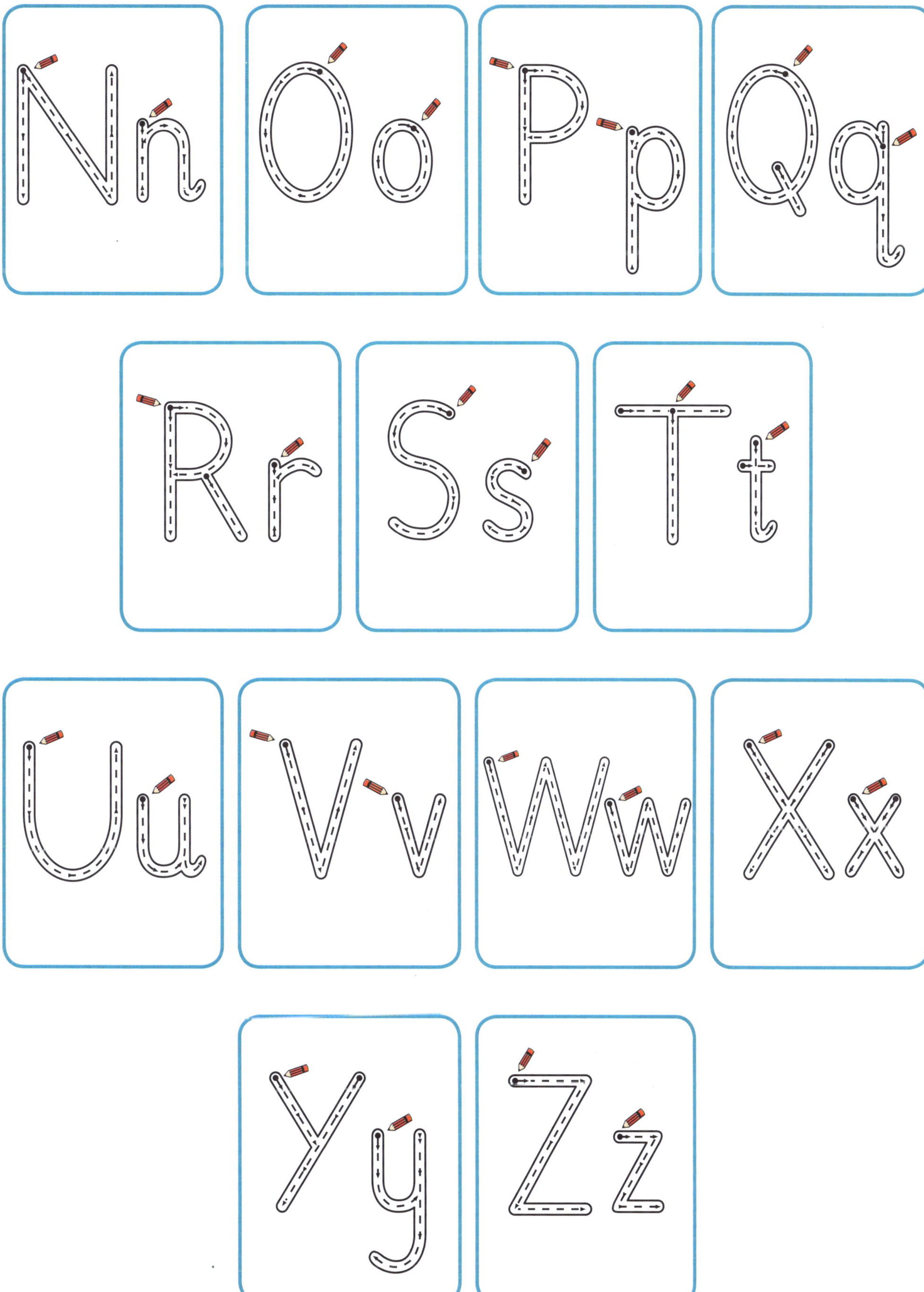

Words with ay

t	r	ay

tray

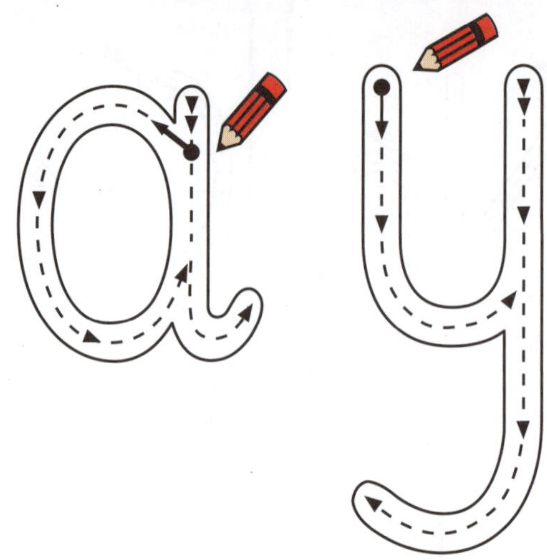

Read the rhyme

Circle **ay** in the rhyme.

I say, I say! Let's play today.
Hop away! Skip away!
May I play today?

Make the words

Make some words. Write the words. Read the words.

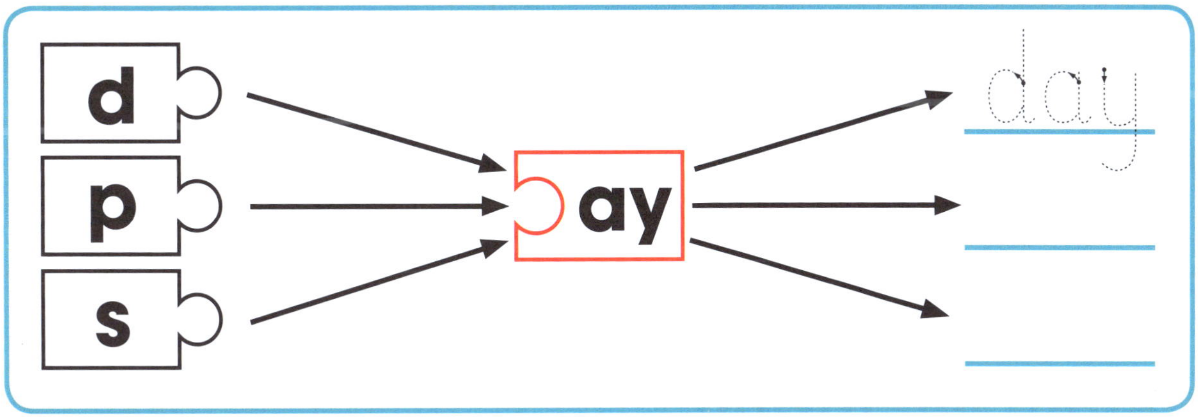

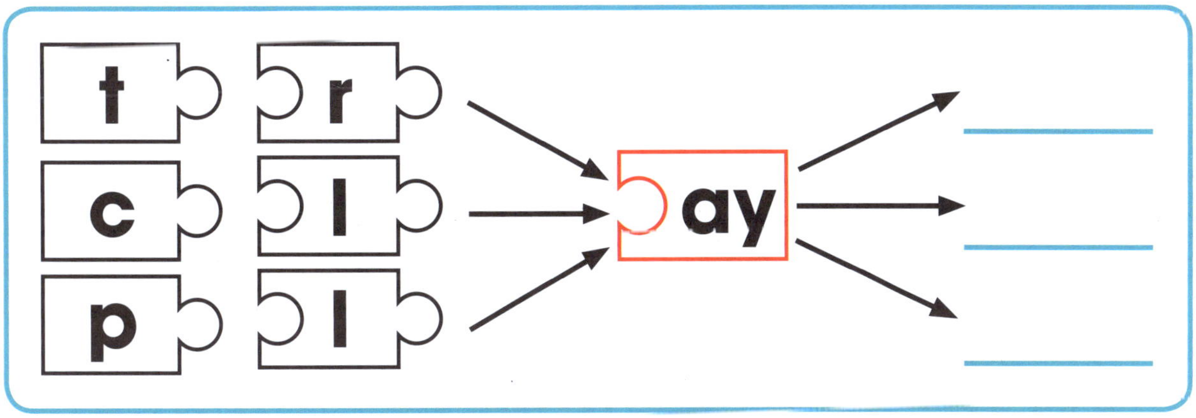

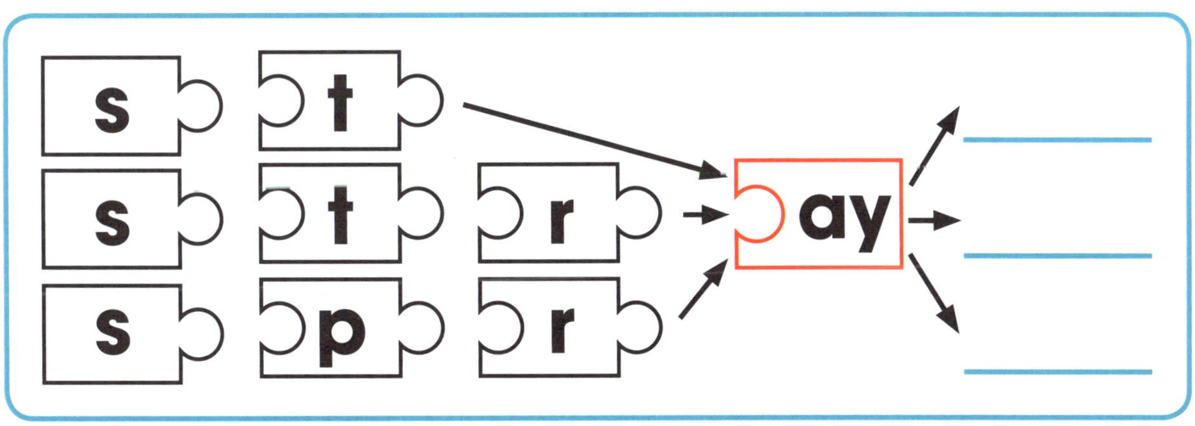

Teacher's tip

Before beginning this page you could encourage the learner to have fun making up rhymes. For example: 'Go away to Bombay', 'Don't play on the motorway', 'Stay on the pathway', 'I'll play with the spray', 'You may carry the tray of clay', 'Play every day', 'There's some hay in the bay'.

Words with ou

Read the rhyme

Circle **ou** in the rhyme.

The roundabout goes round and round.
We bound around the playground.
We shout and shout.
On the roundabout.

Match the words

Read the words.
Match pairs of rhyming words.

Write the words.
Colour **ou** in the words.

shout	south
cloud	spout
sound	pouch
mouth	found
house	proud
couch	mouse

shout spout

Teacher's tip

Read 'shout' and 'spout' aloud (emphasising the 'out' sounds). Ask the learner what he/she notices about the sounds at the ends of the words. Point out the line that joins them 'because they rhyme'. Say the next word in the left-hand ladder ('cloud'), emphasising 'oud'. Tell the learner that there is a rhyming word in the other ladder. Read the words in the right-hand ladder. Ask which word rhymes with 'cloud'.

Words with oy

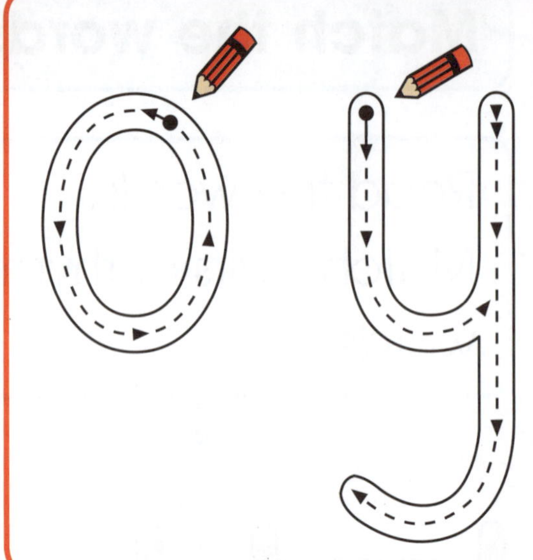

Read the rhyme

Circle **oy** in the rhyme.

Preeti is a girl. Joy is a boy.
They fell out over a toy.
"Let's enjoy it, not destroy it,
Don't annoy me," said Preeti to Joy.

Make the words

Make some words. Read the words.

oy → b___ t___ enj___ ann___

oy → empl___ cowb___ destr___

Write the words

Write the words in the grid.

Put one sound in each box.

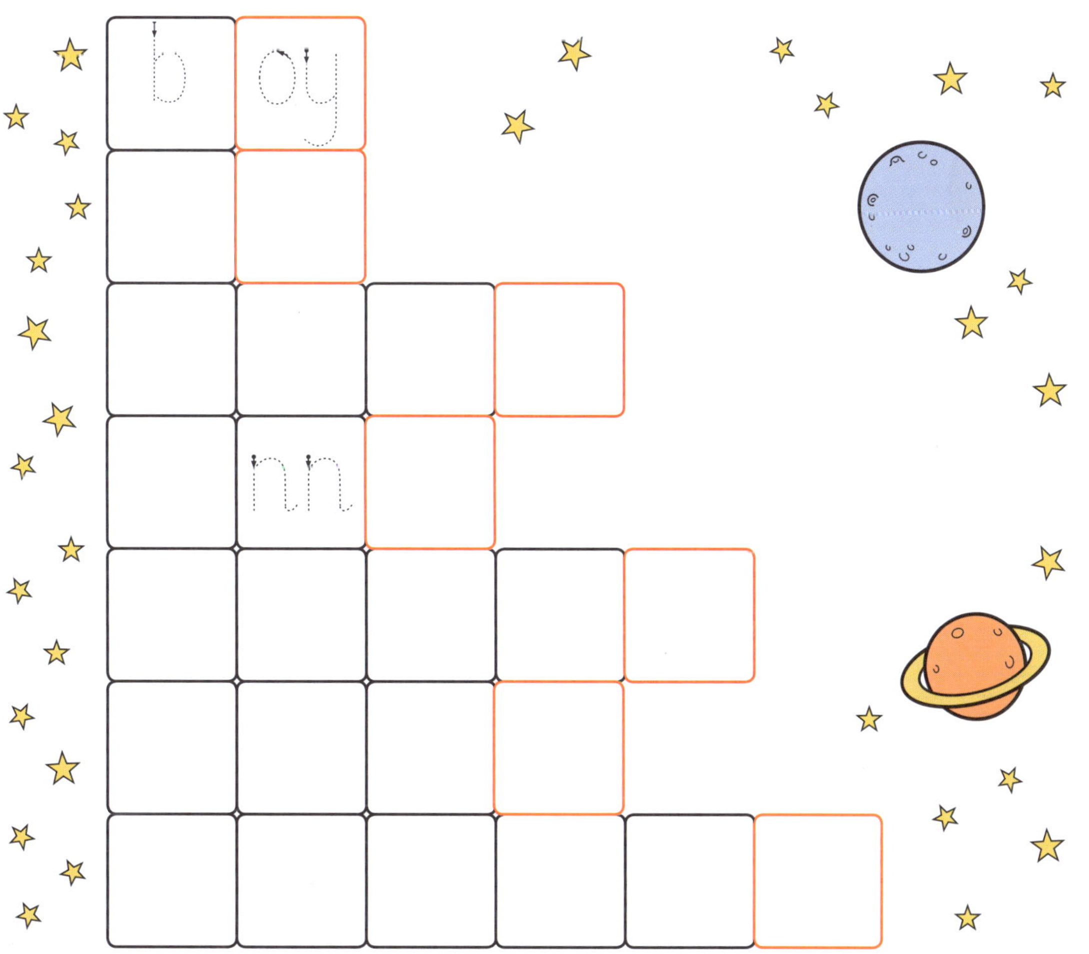

Words with ir

b | ir | d

bird

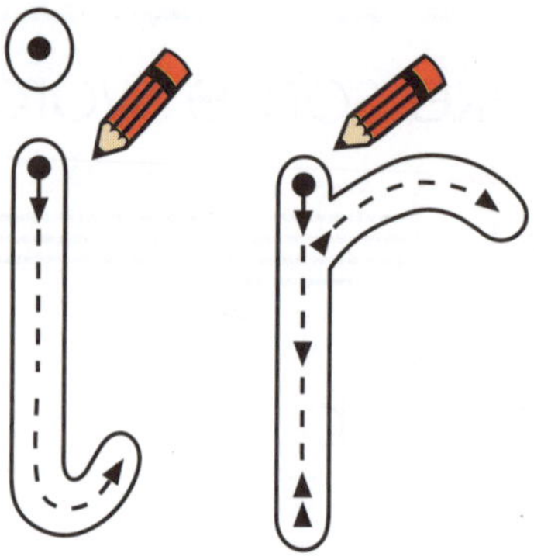

Read the rhyme

Circle **ir** in the rhyme.

The first girl is thirsty.

The second girl's skirt is dirty.

The third girl, I'm glad to say,
is happy on her birthday!

Match the words

Read the words.
Match pairs of rhyming words.

Write the words.
Colour **ir** in the words.

sir	thirst
bird	stir
first	third
skirt	twirl
girl	shirt

sir stir

Teacher's tip

If necessary, explain that there are different ways of spelling the same sound. Write 'ir' and ask the learner to say the sound 'ir' and give some examples of words he/she has learned that have 'ir' in them. Read 'sir' and 'stir' aloud (emphasising the 'ir' sounds). Ask the learner what they notice about the sounds at the ends of the words. Point out the line that joins them 'because they rhyme'. Say the next word in the left-hand ladder ('bird'), emphasising 'ird'. Tell the learner that there is a rhyming word in the other ladder. Read the words in the right-hand ladder. Ask which word rhymes with 'bird'.

Words with ea

b ea ch

beach

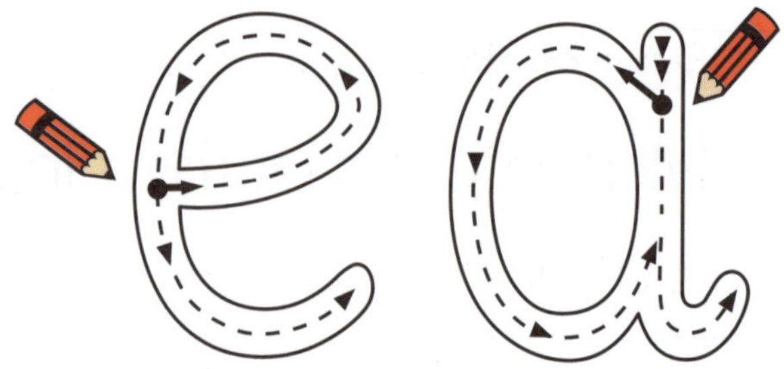

Read the rhyme

Circle **ea** in the rhyme.

Play on the beach.

Swim in the sea.

Sit on a seat.

Eat your tea!

Read the words

Read the words. Write the words.

ea → t eat	s → ea → l	r → ea → d
t → ea → ch	l → ea → p	b → ea → k

Write the words

Write the correct word under each picture.

Words with aw

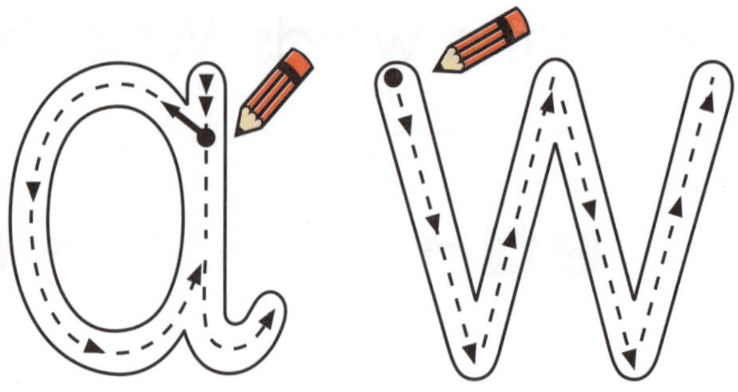

Read the rhyme

Circle **aw** in the rhyme.

We hammer and saw.

We paint and draw.

I have four paws.

I grip with my claws.

Read the words

Read the words. Write the words.

s → aw saw	l → aw → n	d → r → aw
h → aw → k	th → aw	f → aw → n

Write the words

Write the correct word under each picture.

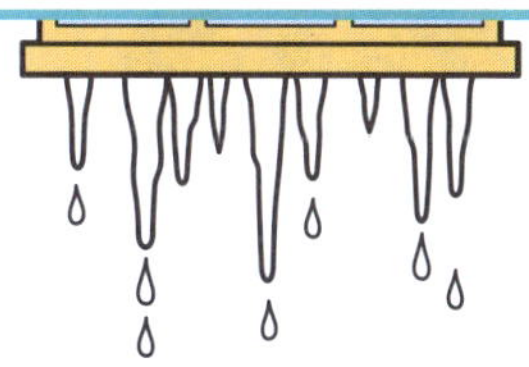

Words with ew

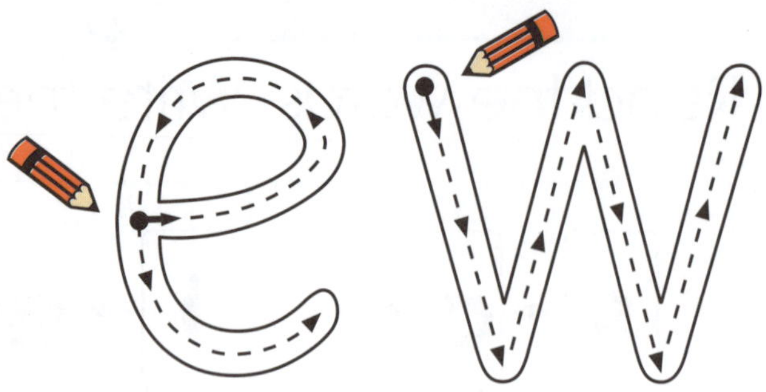

Read the rhyme

Circle **ew** in the rhyme.

Make the words

Make the words. Write the words. Read the words.

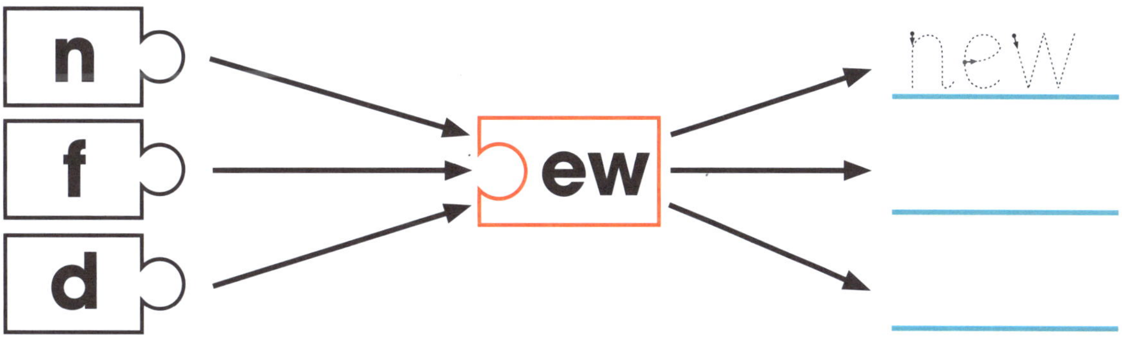

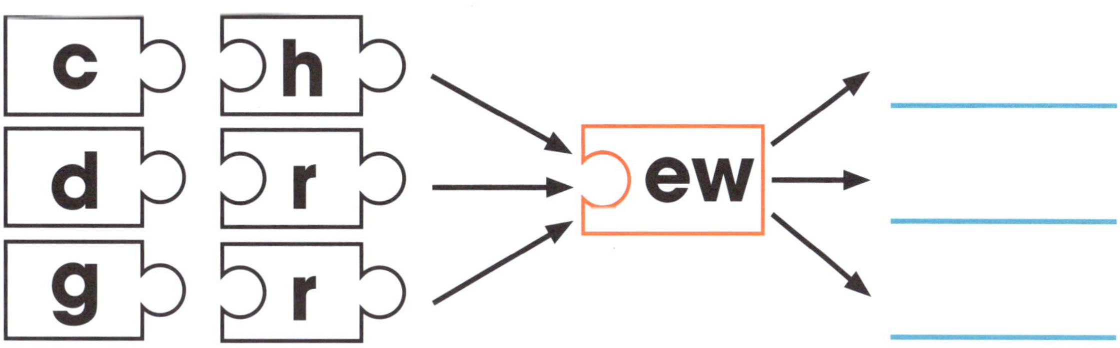

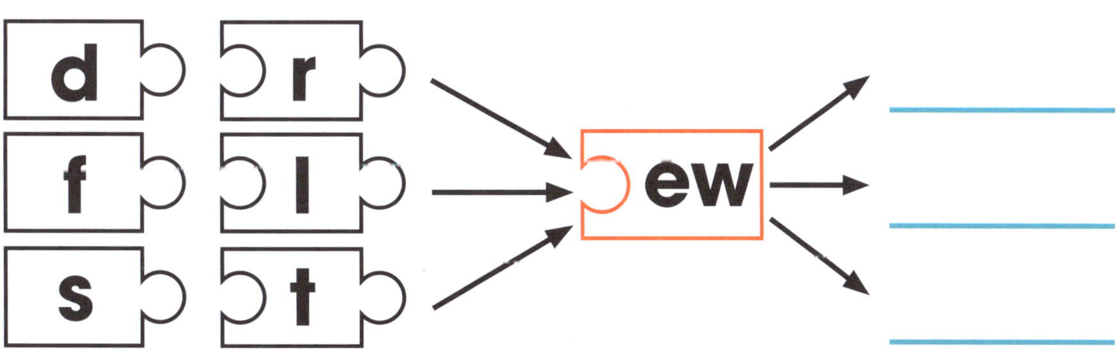

Teacher's tip

If necessary, explain that there are different ways of spelling the same sound. Write 'ew' and ask the learner to say the sound 'ew' and give some examples of words he/she has learned that have 'ew' in them. For example: chew, grew, flew, drew, threw.

Words with ue

Make the words

Make some words and names. Read the words.

ue → bl____ gl____ tr____ cr____l

ue → T____sday val____ resc____

Write the words

Write the words in the grid. Put one sound in each box.

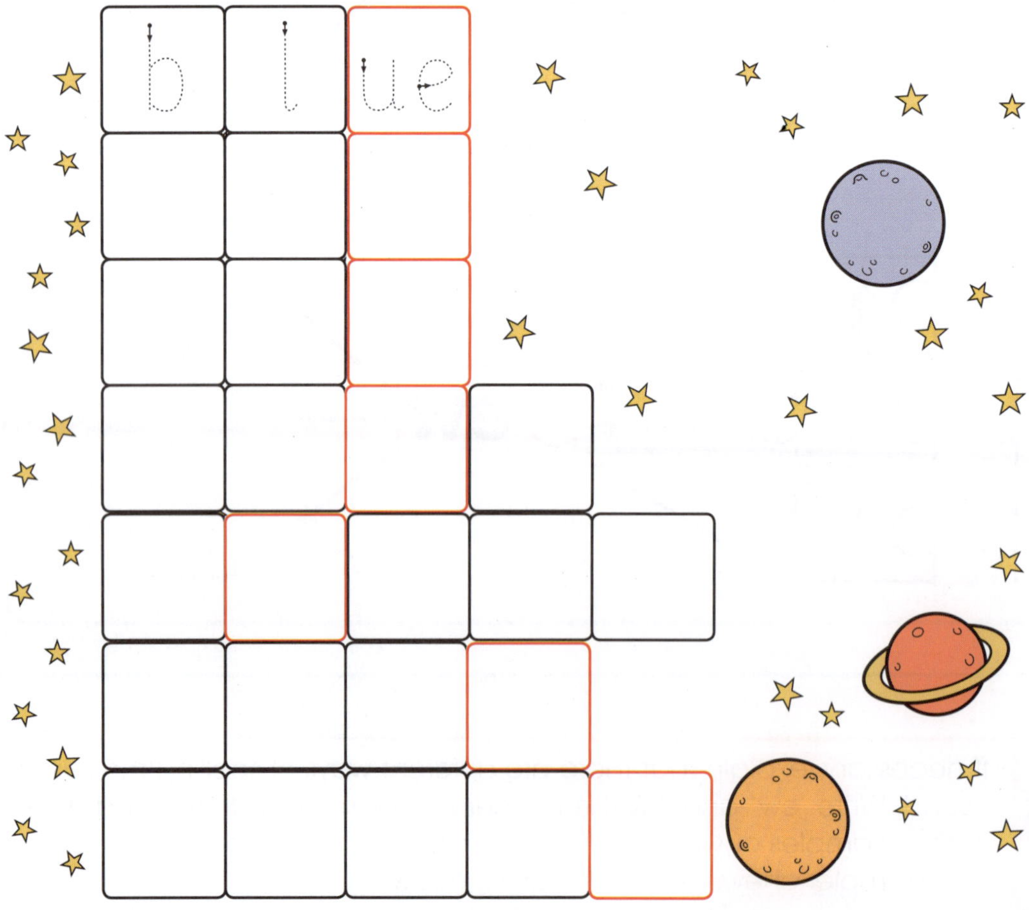

Make the words

Make some words and names. Read the words.

oe

t___ d___ f___ h___

oe

w___ J___ g___s

Write the words

Write the words in the grid. Put one sound in each box.

t oe

Words with au

Make the words

Make some words and names. Read the words.

au → P___l   h___l   s___ce   s___cer

au → l___nch   ___gust   h___nt

Write the words

Write the words in the grid. Put one sound in each box.

P	au	l		

Make the words

Make some words with **ie**. Read the words.

ie → p____ d____ t____ d____d

ie → l____s cr____d t____d

Write the words

Write the words in the grid. Put one sound in each box.

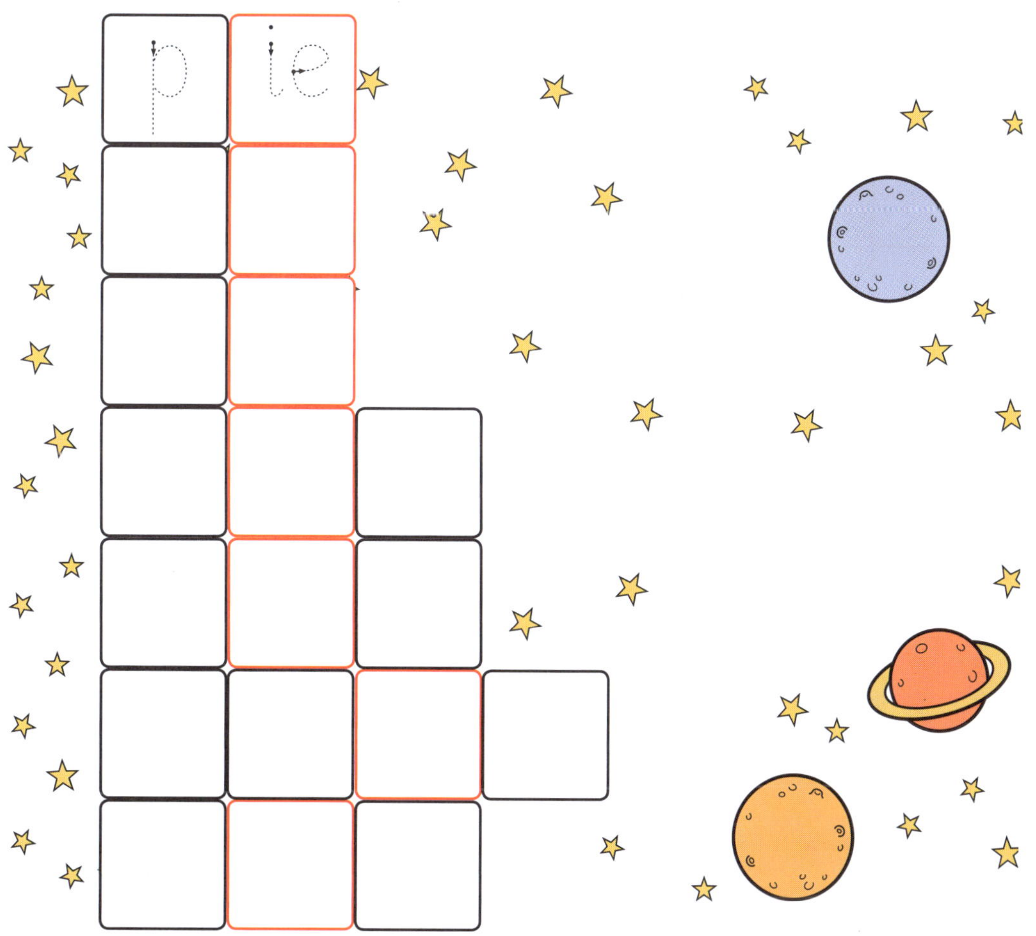

When ey says ay

Make some words

Make some words with **ey**. Read the words.

ey

H____ th____ gr____ ob____

Hey! **ey** can sound like **ay**!

Write the words

Write the words in the grid. Put one sound in each box.

H	

My nest is a dr____.

k ey

key

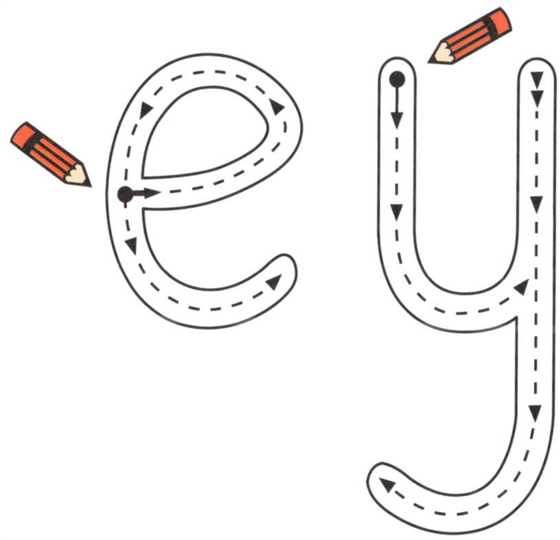

Make the words

Make the words with **ey**.

Read the words. Write the words.

m o n ___ → ________

j o ck ___ → ________

d o n k ___ → ________

t ur k ___ → ________

ch i m n ___ → ________

Split digraph a-e

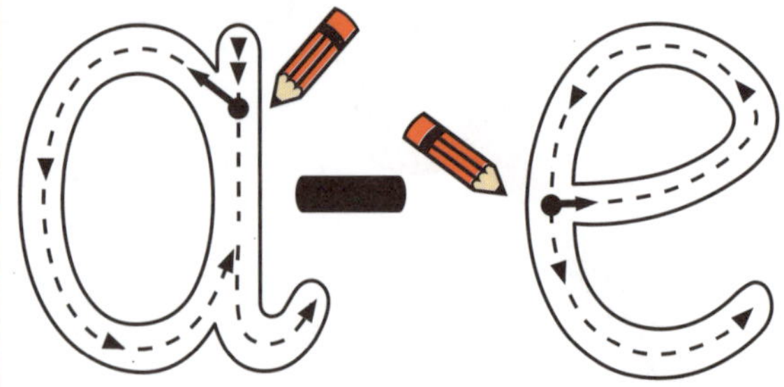

Read the story

Colour **a-e** in the story. Join **a-e**.

1

Wake up.

2

Make the bed.

3

Shake the mat.

4

Rake the leaves.

5

Bake a cake.

6

Take a nap!

Write the words

Write the a-e words.

f a c e

w _ _ _

_ _ _ _

Match the words

Match up the rhyming words.

made	sale
gale	skate
name	spade
plate	mane
lane	save
cave	tame

Write the words. Read the words.

made spade

Split digraph i-e

s m i l e

smile

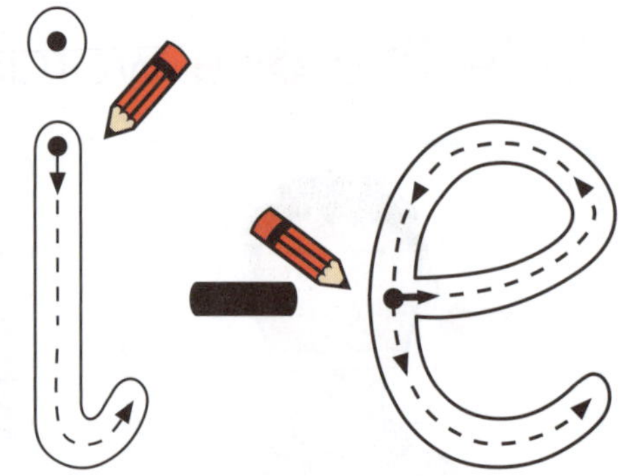

Read the rhyme

Colour **i-e** in the rhyme. Join **i-e**.

Sail down the Nile,
And after a mile
You will see a crocodile
With a fine smile!

Write the words

Write the i-e words.

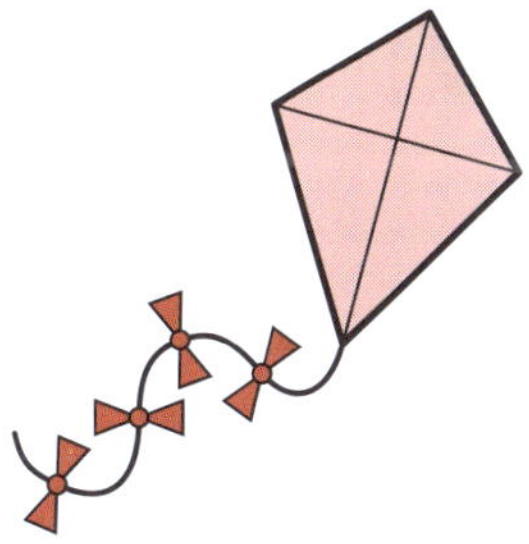

b i k e

Match the words

Match up the rhyming words.

Write the words. Read the words.

ride	spike
like	wise
time	stripe
wipe	hive
rise	slide
dive	chime

ride slide

Split digraph o-e

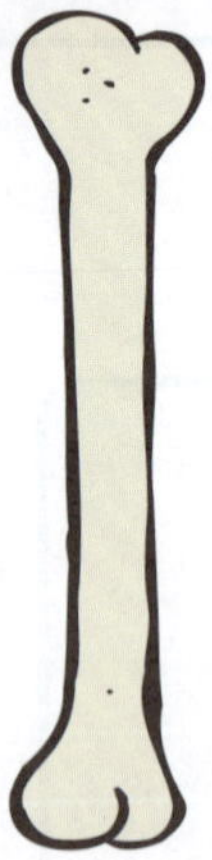

b o n e

bone

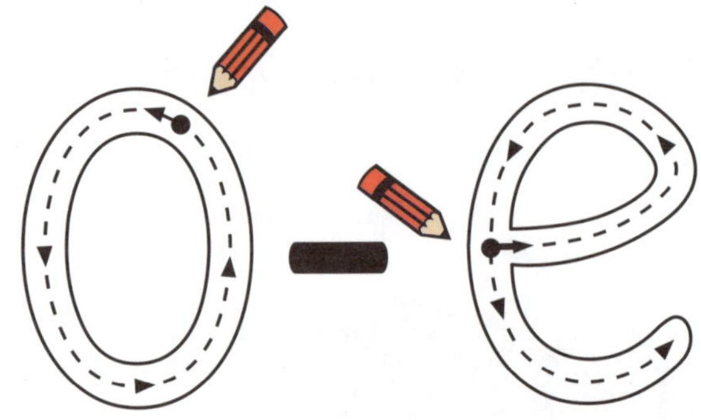

Read the rhyme

Colour **o-e** in the rhyme. Join **o-e**.

Old King Cole
Fell down a hole.
He broke a bone
On a big stone.

Write the words

Write the o-e words.

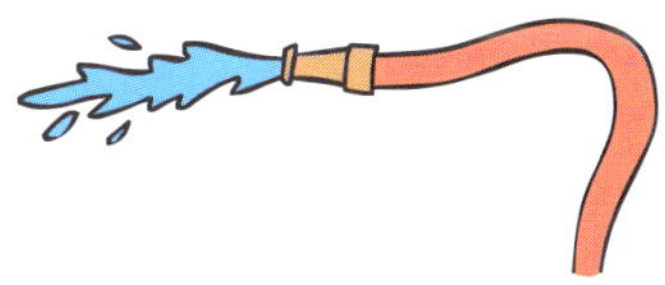

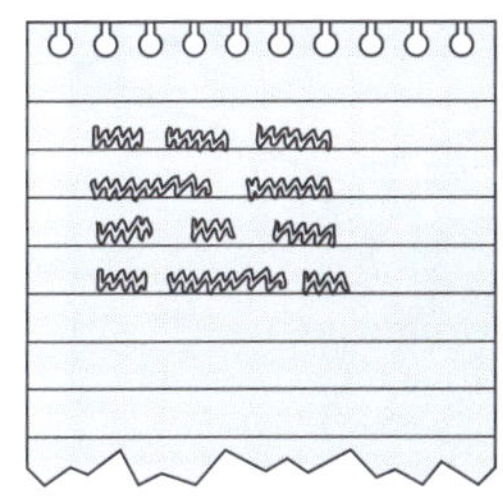

c o n e

Match the words

Match up the rhyming words.

Write the words. Read the words.

nose	rope
joke	stole
hope	dome
bone	poke
home	close
pole	stone

nose close

Split digraph u-e

c u b e

cube

u-e

Read the rhyme

Colour **u-e** in the rhyme. Join **u-e**.

Duke Luke plays a tune on his flute.

Write the words

Write the u-e words.

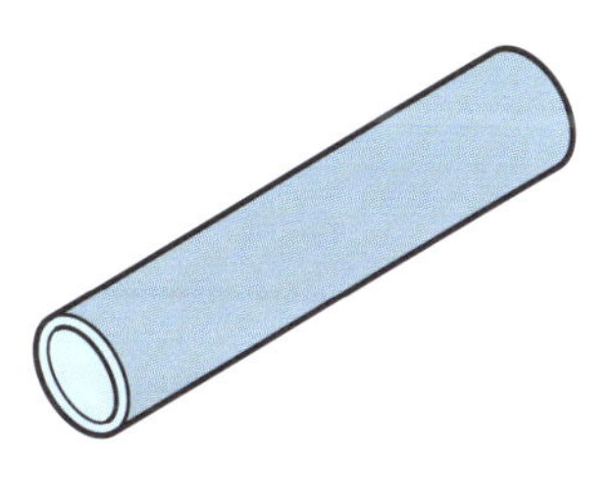  

t u b e

Match the words

Match up the rhyming words.

Write the words. Read the words.

cube	June
tune	fuse
rule	Luke
use	flute
cute	tube
duke	mule

tube → cube tube

Split digraph e-e

e | v | e | n | i | n | g

evening

P | e | t | e

Pete

My name is Pete.

Make the words

Make the words and names with **e-e**.
Read the words. Write the words.

th | | s | → ______

th | | m | → ______

S | t | | v | → ______

e | x | t | r | | m | → ______

c | o | n | c | r | | t | → ______

Complete the words

Complete the words with **i**. Read the words.
Write the words.

f	i	n	d

m		n	d

b		n	d

Make the words

Make the words with **i**.
Read the words. Write the words.

ch		l	d	→	______
w		l	d	→	______
k		n	d	→	______
	b	e	x	→	______

b	e	h		n	d	→	______

When a says ar

b	a	th

bath

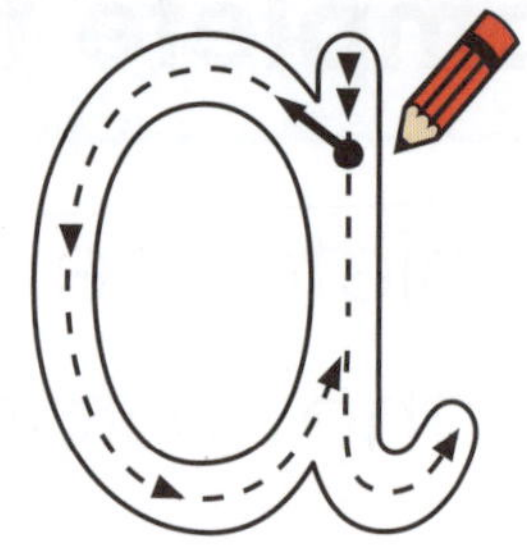

Write the word

Write the word for each picture. Read the words.

r	a	f	t

m			

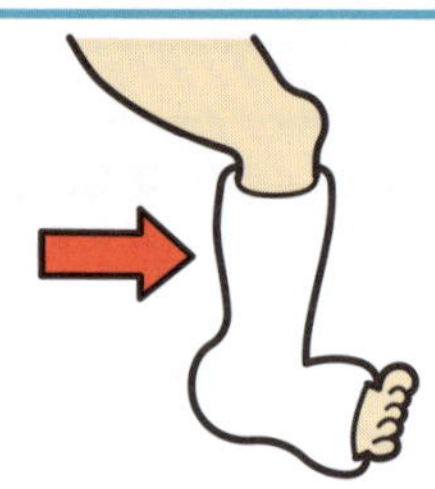

c			

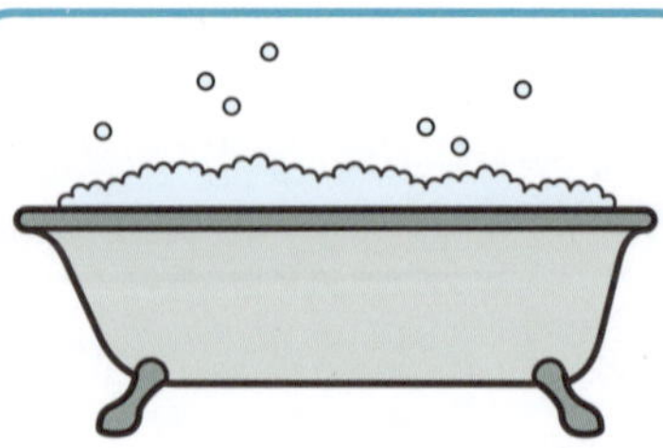

a	c	or	n

acorn

Make the words

Make the words with **a**.

Read the words. Write the words.

	p	r	o	n		→ ______
	p	r	i	l		→ ______
b		s	i	n		→ ______
m		s	o	n		→ ______
	p	r	i	c	o	t → ______

Teacher's tip

Remind the learner that names start with a capital letter.

A different u sound

Read the rhyme

Circle **u** in the rhyme.

Never pull or push
A bull in a bush.
For if you do,
It may push you, too!

Choose the word

Choose the correct word for each picture.

full | pull

____

pull | bull

____

bush | push

____

push | put

____

bull | bush

____

pull | push

____

When o says u

Write the words

Write the word for each picture.
They all rhyme.

love

d

Match the words

Match the rhyming words.

Write the words. Read the words.

some	mother
money	none
done	honey
other	come

Write the name of a day of the week with **o**.

When er rhymes with her

g	er	m

germ

f	er	n

fern

Make the words

Make the words with **er**.

Read the words. Write the words.

j		k	→ ______
t		m	→ ______
k		b	→ ______
s t		n	→ ______
p		ch	→ ______

When ow says oh

s **n** **ow**

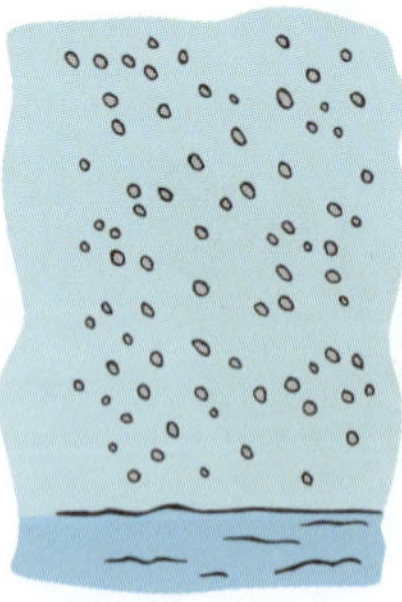

snow

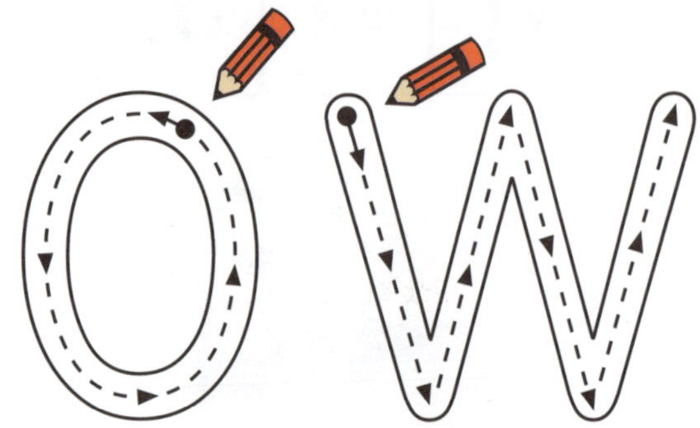

Read the rhyme

Circle **ow** in the rhyme.

I can row.

I can mow.

I can blow.

I can grow!

Teacher's tip The learner might know words in which 'ow' represents the 'ow' sound in 'cow'. Point out that 'ow' can be used for a different sound – in glow, show, grow, snow and many other words.

Swap the sound

Read the words.	Swap the first sound for:	Write the words. Read the words.
low	m	mow
tow	r	
crow	g	
blow	s	
glow	f	
grow	c	
follow	h	
borrow	s	
yellow	b	
pillow	w	
narrow	b	

When ie says ee

Write the words

Write the words with **ie**. Read the words.

ch	ie	f

th	ie	f

b	r	ie	f

______ ______ ______

Make the words

Make the words with **ie**.

Read the words. Write the words.

f		l	d

→ ______

sh		l	d

→ ______

p	r		s	t

→ ______

sh	r		k

→ ______

b	e	l		f

→ ______

When y says ee

j	e	ll	y

jelly

m	u	mm	y

mummy

Make the words

Make the words with **y**.

Read the words. Write the words.

j	o	ll		→	______
l	a	z		→	______
h	a	pp		→	______
oi	l			→	______
e	v	er		→	______

When ea says e

b r ea d

bread

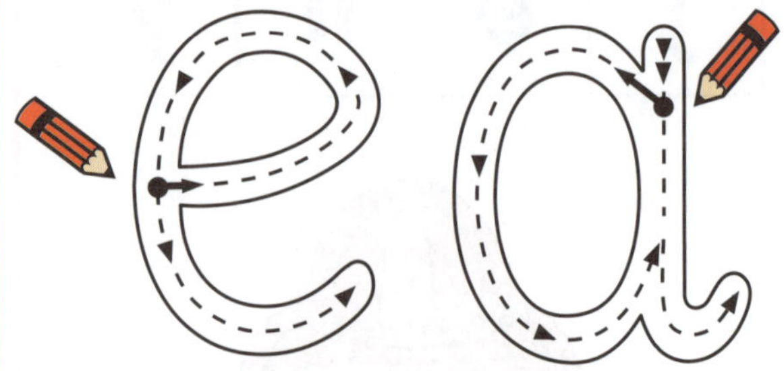

Read the rhyme

Circle **ea** in the rhyme.

The little bird is pecking for bread.
Bob, bob, bob goes its head.
It flaps its wings and shakes its feathers.
It visits my garden in all kinds of weather.

Swap the sound

Read the words.	Swap the first sound for:	Write the words.
head	d	dead
bread	d	
thread	s p	
feather	w	
leather	h	
ready	s t	
healthy	w	
death	b r	

Teacher's tip The learner might know words in which 'ea' represents the 'ea' sound (like ee) in 'meat'. Point out that 'ea' can be used for a different sound – in dead, bread, head, deaf and many other words.

When y says igh

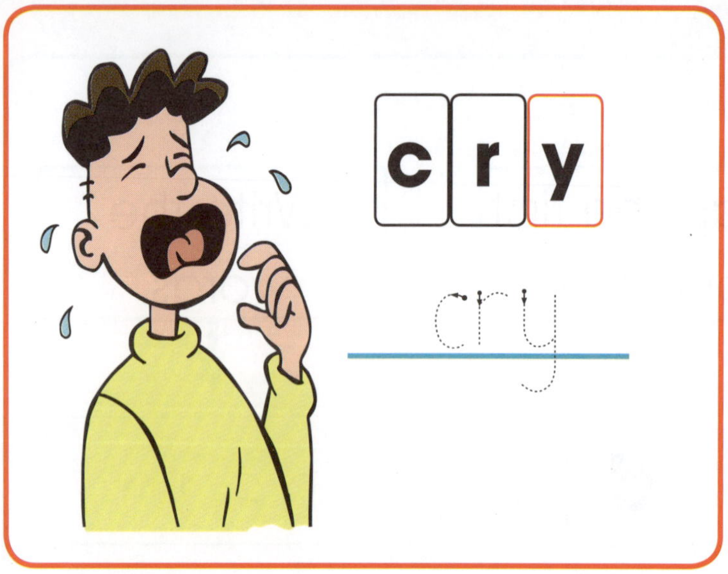

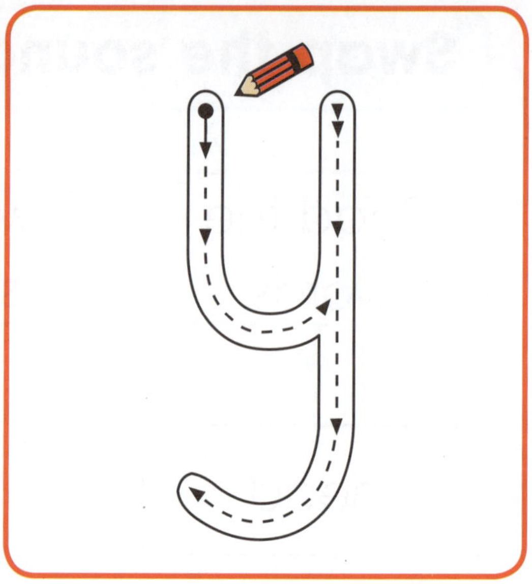

Read the rhyme

Circle **y** in the rhyme.

Why do you cry? Why do you cry?
Soon you'll be a butterfly.
And flutter by in the sky!

Make the words

Make the **y** words.

Read the words. Write the words.

y

m___ sh___ sl___ sp___

my ______ ______ ______

y

dr___ fr___ tr___ repl___

______ ______ ______ ______

y

den___ sk___ dragonfl___

______ ______ ______

Teacher's tip

The learner might know words in which 'y' represents the 'y' sound (like ee) in 'silly'. Point out that 'y' can be used for a different sound – in sky, my, by, try and many other words.

When or says ur

w | or | m

worm

w | or | l | d

world

Make the words

Make the words with **or**.

Read the words. Write the words.

w | ___ | d → ____________

w | ___ | k → ____________

w | ___ | th → ____________

w | ___ | s | t → ____________

w | ___ | sh | i | p → ____________

When al says ar

p | al | m

palm

al | m | o | n | d

almond

Make the words

Make the words with **al**.

Read the words. Write the words.

c | | f → ______

h | | f → ______

c | | m → ______

l | i | p | b | | m → ______

When ear says er

Read the rhyme

Circle **ear** in the rhyme.

Teddy bear, teddy bear,
Your coat has a tear.
Teddy bear, teddy bear,
What will you wear?

Make the words

Make some words. Write the words.

b, t, w, p → **ear** →

bear

____

____

____

Use the words to fill in the crossword.

Down

1. A large wild animal
2. To dress in something

Across

3. A kind of fruit
4. To rip something

When are says air

s | qu | are

square

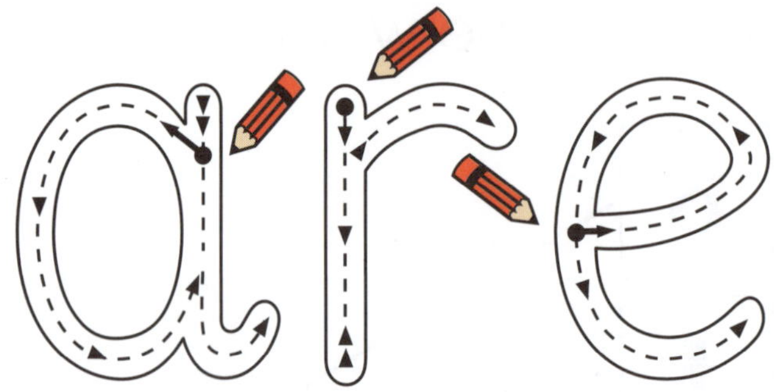

Read the rhyme

Circle **are** in the rhyme.

Once I saw a rare hare.
"Stare at me if you dare," said the hare.
"I don't care!"
I have stares to spare.

Make the words

Make some words with **are**. Read the words.
Write the words.

are

b______ c______ d______

bare

are

r______ h______ m______

are

sh______ sc______ sp______

are

st______ squ______ bew______

Words with eer

d eer

deer

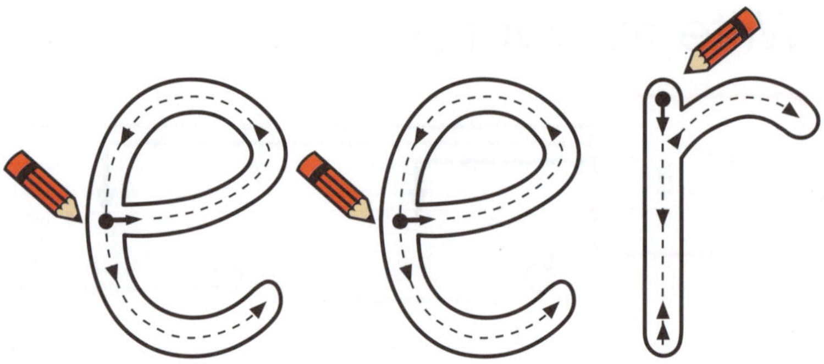

Make the words

Make the words with **eer**.

Read the words. Write the words.

j ______ → ______

p ______ → ______

sh ______ → ______

s t ______ → ______

Teacher's tip Practise saying the 'eer' sound in 'deer' with the learner. Explain that all the words have this sound and that even if the learner hasn't seen or heard these words before he/she can read them by sounding the letters.

Words with ear or eer

Sort the words

Read the words.

Sort the words into sets.

ear words	**eer** words

Words with oor

d oor

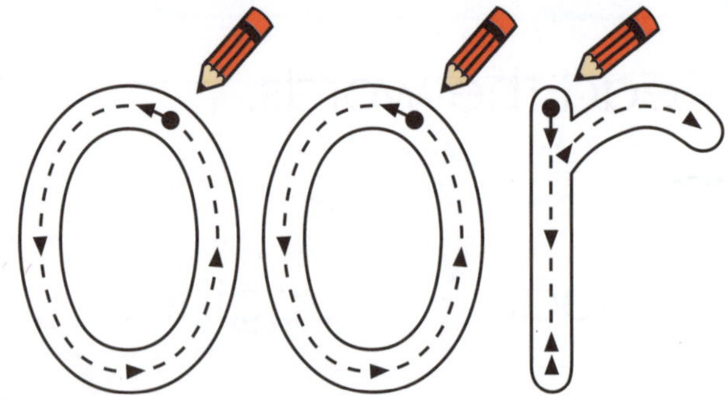

Make the words

Make the words with **oor**.

Read the words. Write the words.

d ___ → ______

m ___ → ______

p ___ → ______

f l ___ → ______

t a n d ___ i → ______

Join the words

Make words from door + another word.
Write the words.

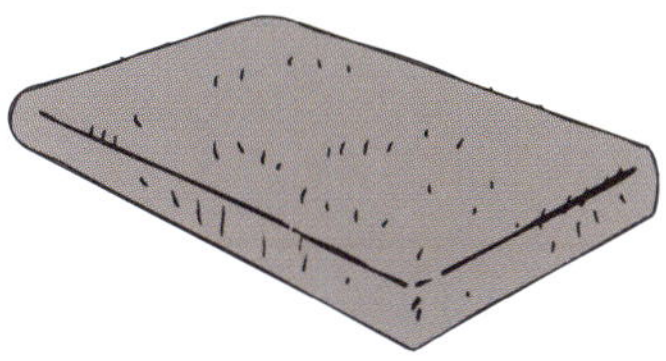

doormat

_______man

_______way

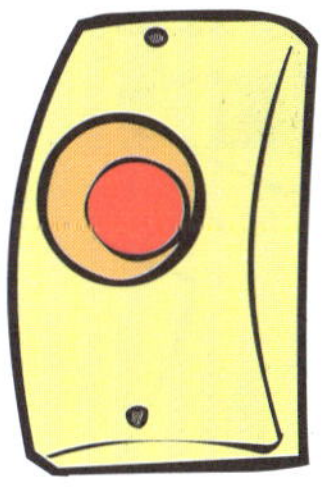

_______bell

_______step

trap_______

Teacher's tip

Point out to the learner that they have learned different ways of spelling the sound 'or'. Revisit page 64 and ask the learner to read the word at the top of the page. Ask which letters spell the sound 'or'.

Tell the learner that the words on this page have 'oor' in them. When the learner has written the words, ask him/her to read them.

Words with ore

s | c | ore

score

ore

Read the rhyme

Circle **ore** in the rhyme.

Snore! Snore! Snore!
I can't stand it any more.
I've told Father before
That his snore is a bore!

Make the words

Make some words with **ore**. Read the words.

ore

c___ t___ ch___ st___

ore

sh___ ign___ expl___

Write the words

Write the words in the grid. Put one sound in each box.

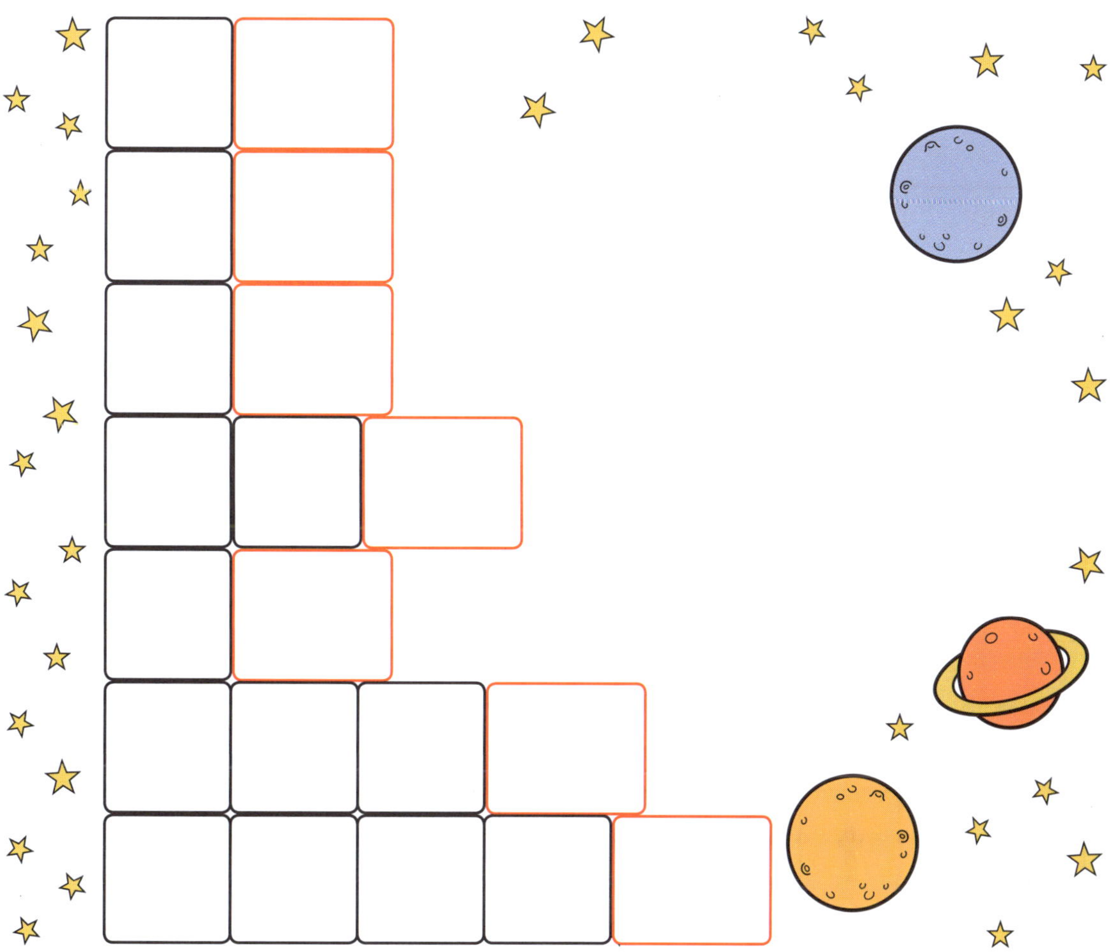

Words with our

p | our

pour

c | our | t

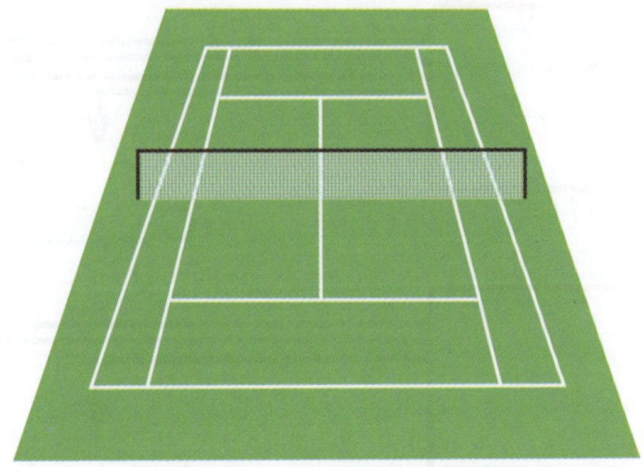

court

Make the words

Make the words with **our**.

Read the words. Write the words.

y | ___ → ______

f | ___ → ______

f | ___ | th → ______

f | ___ | t | ee | n → ______

c | ___ | t | y | ar | d → ______

Words with augh

d	augh	t	er

daughter

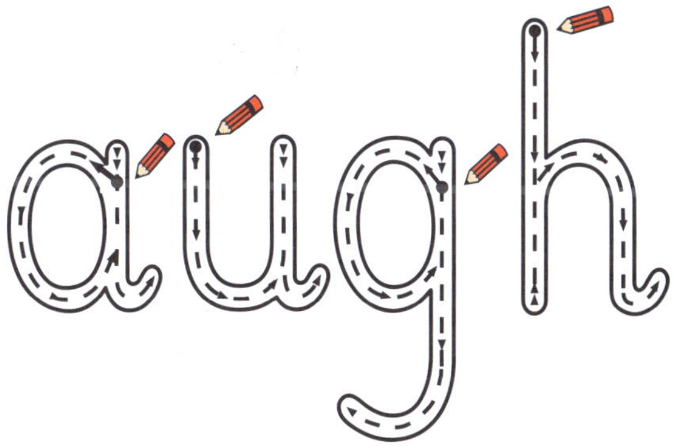

Make the words

Make the words with **augh**.

Read the words. Write the words.

d		t	er	→ ______
n		t	y	→ ______
c		t		→ ______
t		t		→ ______

s	l		t	er	→ ______

Words with al

w	al	k

walk

t	al	k

talk

Make the words

Make the words with **al**.

Read the words. Write the words.

ch		k	→ ______

s	t		k	→ ______

w		k	er	→ ______

b	ea	n	s	t		k	→ ______

s	i	d	e	w		k	→ ______

Words with all

b	all

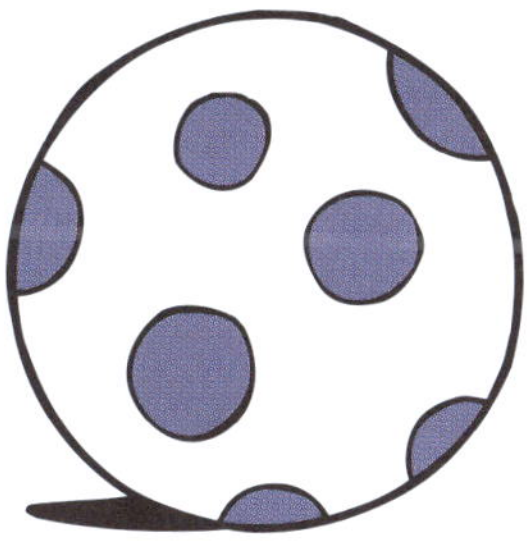

ball

w	all

wall

Make the words

Make the words with **all**.

Read the words. Write the words.

c [ ] → ______

t [ ] → ______

f [ ] → ______

s m [ ] → ______

s t [ ] → ______

Words with wh

Read the words

Read the words that begin **wh**. Circle **wh** in the words.

Write two questions:

When ____________________

Why ____________________

Make the words

Make some words with **wh**. Write the words.

Read the words.

wh	en	→	when
	ip	→	
	y	→	
	ere	→	
	at	→	
	ich	→	

wh	ite	→	white
	ile	→	
	am	→	
	ack	→	
	eat	→	
	isper	→	

Teacher's tip

Ask the learner which letter to use for the sound 'w' (say the sound, not the letter name). He/she should know that the letter is 'w'. Then ask if he/she knows how to spell 'when'. If so, point out the letters 'wh'. Tell him/her that there are a few words that have 'wh' for the 'w' sound.

Words with ph

ph	o	n	e

phone

Read the rhyme

Circle **ph** in the rhyme.

We call the alphabet
the ABC.

Elephants eat leaves from
a tree.

Dolphins swim in the deep
blue sea.

All my friends phone me!

Make the words

Make some words with **ph**. Read the words.
Write the words.

ph

____oto　　____one　　gra____

photo　　______　　______

ph

dol____in　　ele____ant　　al____abet

______　　______　　______

Write the words

Write the correct word under each picture.

______

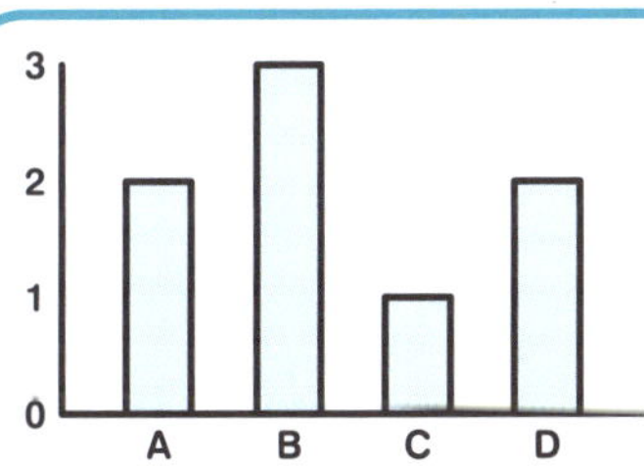

______

______

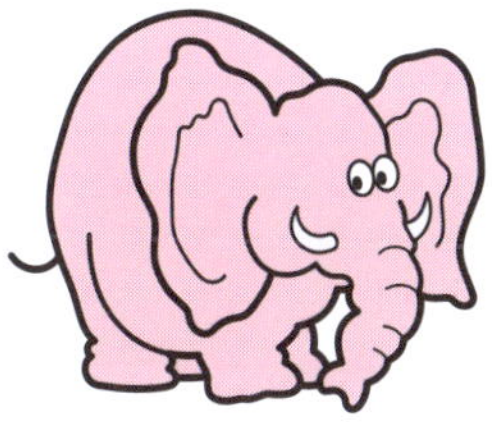
______

______

______

Words with tch

c	r	u	tch

crutch

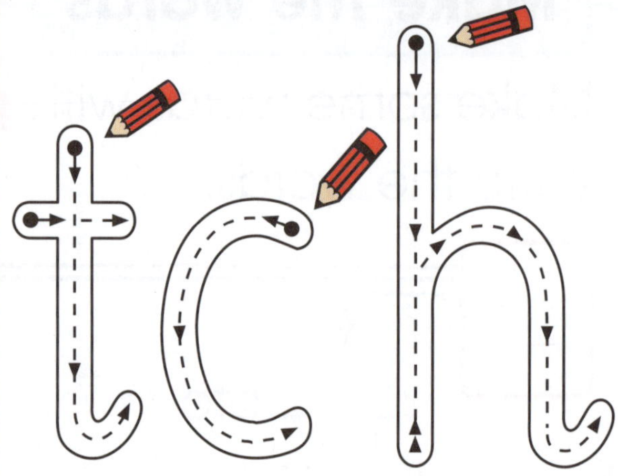

Read the rhyme

Circle **tch** in the rhyme.

We're all at the match.
See that catch!
Bowling down the pitch.
Oh, no! He's in the ditch!

Make the words

Make some words with **tch**. Read the words.

tch → ha___ sti___ swi___ ske___

tch → hu___ bu___er ke___up

Write the words

Write the words in the grid. Put one sound in each box.

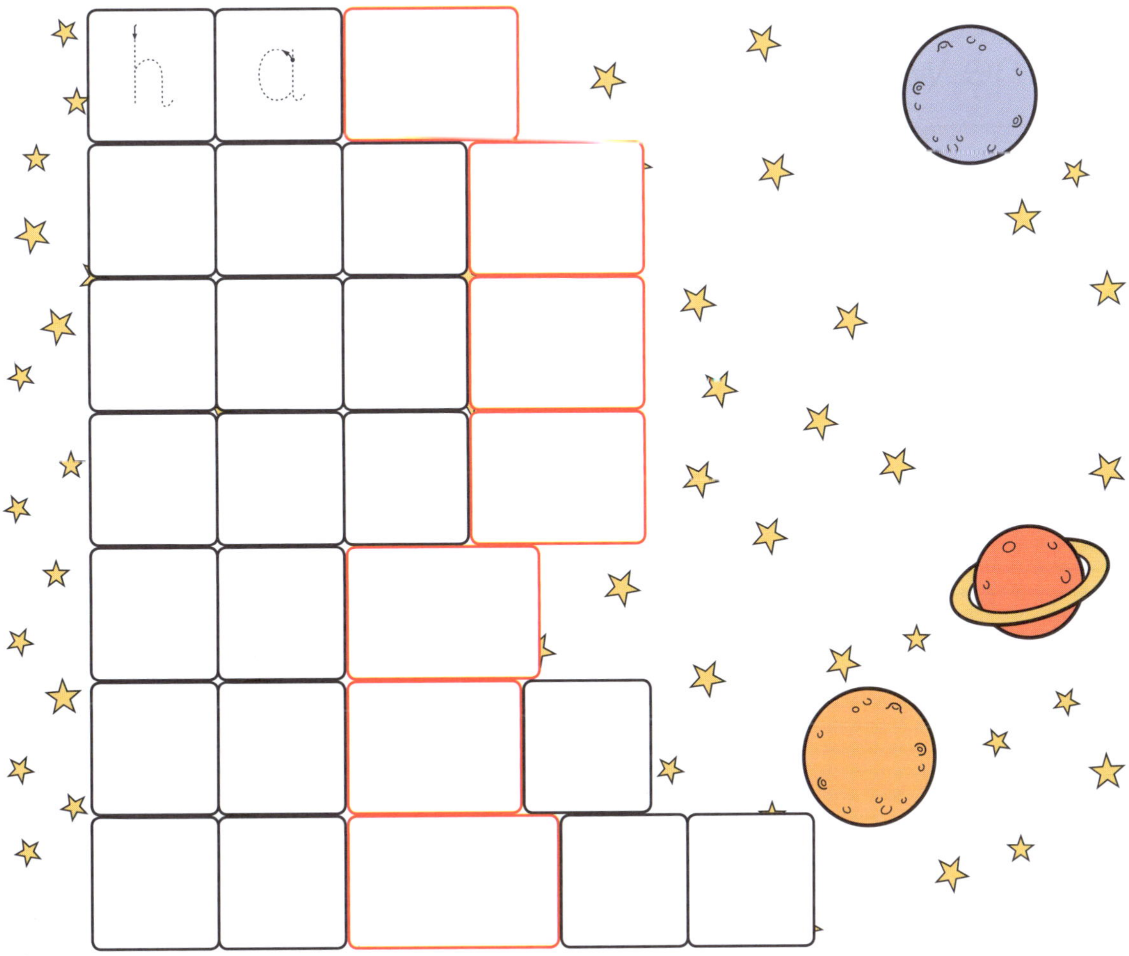

Words with dge

j	u	dge

judge

b	r	i	dge

bridge

Make the words

Make the words with **dge**.

Read the words. Write the words.

d	o			→	______
h	e			→	______
f	u			→	______
b	a			→	______
b	a		er	→	______

When tu says ch

p	i	c	tu	re

picture

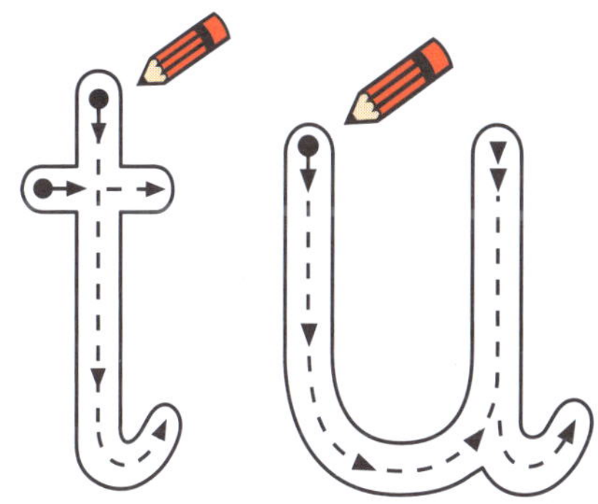

Make the words

Make the words with **tu**.

Read the words. Write the words.

n	a		re	→ ______
c	a	p		re → ______
f	u		re	→ ______
m	i	x		re → ______
p	u	n	c	re → ______

When ch says k

s	ch	oo	l

school

Read the rhyme

Circle **ch** in the rhyme.

One day at home I baked a cake,
But it gave me a stomach ache!
I had to go to the chemist shop
For something to make my stomach ache stop!

Make the words

Complete each word with **ch**.
Read the words.

e ___ o	s ___ ool	an ___ or
___ oir	stoma ___	___ emist

Write the words

Write the correct word under each picture.

___

___

___

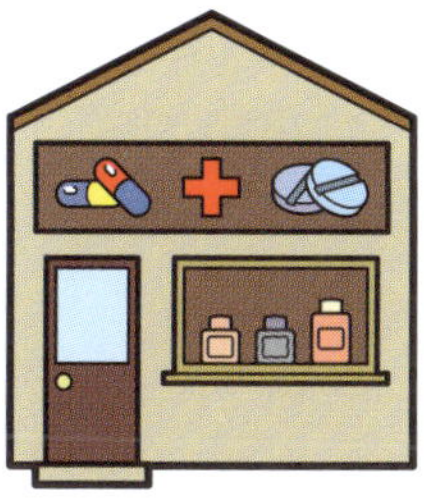
___

___

___

When g says j

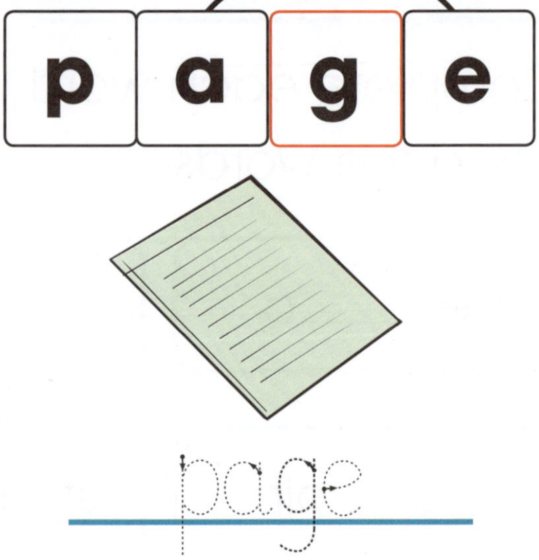

Read the rhyme

Circle **g** that says j in the rhyme.

Raj and Dhiraj live on a barge.
But the barge isn't large.
So it's not at all strange.
That they fancy a change.

Write the words

Write the word for each picture. Read the words.

an____________

g____________

ma____________

dan____________

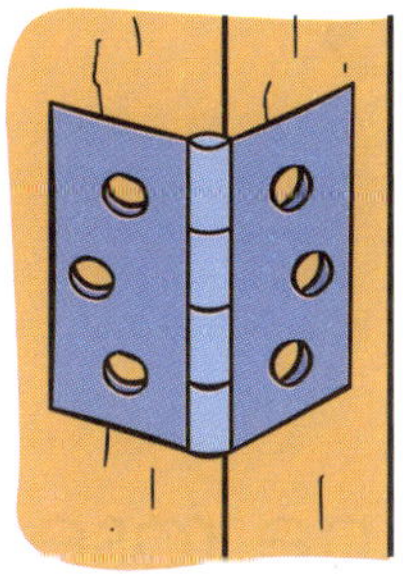

hin____________

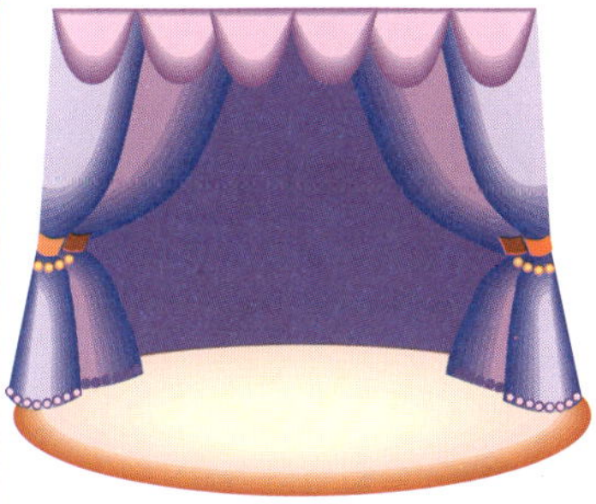

sta____________

Write the words with **g** that says j.
Circle **g** in the words.

A room in a house loun____________

The front of your hair frin____________

Anger ra____________

When s says z

r o s e

rose

h o s e

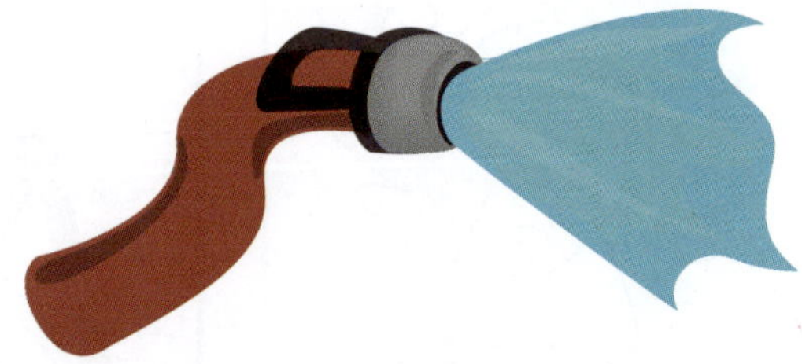

hose

Read the rhyme

Circle **s** in the rhyme.

The rose grows if I use
the hose.

My nose knows when
the rose grows!

I suppose the rose knows
when I use the hose.

Write the words

Read the clues.

Write the words with **s** that says z.

Read the words.

A food made from milk. ch______

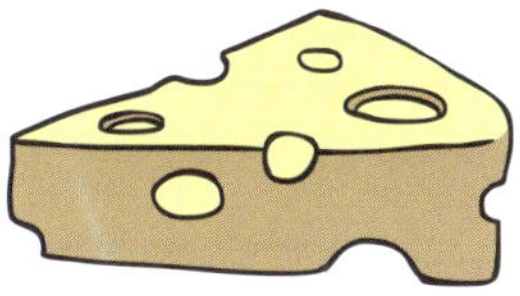

Not hard to do. ea______

A loud sound. n______

A girl's shirt. blou______

A polite word. plea______

To take your pick. ch______

Teacher's tip Write the letter 's' and ask what sound it says. The learner should know the 's' sound as in 'see', 'sit', etc. Tell him/her that in some words 's' says the same sound as 'z'. Write and say some examples. For example: use, rise, rose, nose.

When c says s

c e ll

cell

l a c e

lace

Read the rhyme

Circle **c** that says s in the rhyme.

Charu went to the cinema
On an icy day in December.
She had no lock for her bicycle
So she tied it to an icicle.

Write the words

Read the clues.

Write the words with **c** that says s.

Read the words.

More than one mouse. mi______

This is a smiley f______.

A food that goes with curry. r______

White stuff spread on a cake. i______

You roll these to get a score. d______

You run fast in a r______.

When ci says sh

o p t i **ci** a n

optician

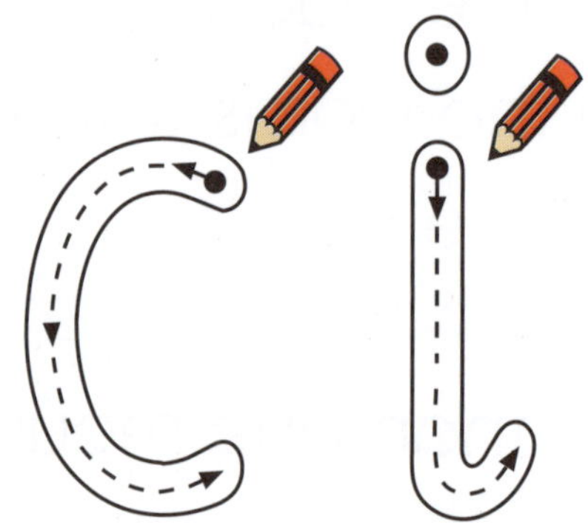

Make the words

Make the words with **ci** that says sh. Write the words. Read the words.

o p t i [ ] a n → ______

s o [ ] a l → ______

s p e [ ] a l → ______

m u s i [ ] a n → ______

When si and su say zh

t e l e v i si o n

television

d i v i si o n

division

Read the rhyme

Circle **s** that says zh in the rhyme.

I look for treasure.
It's a pleasure
To measure the treasure.

When gn says n

s	i	gn

sign

gn	o	m	e

gnome

Make the words

Make the words with **gn** that says n.
Read the sentences.

A [ ] a t is an insect that bites.

A dog will [ ] aw a bone.

If it's angry it might [ ] a sh its teeth.

kn | i | t

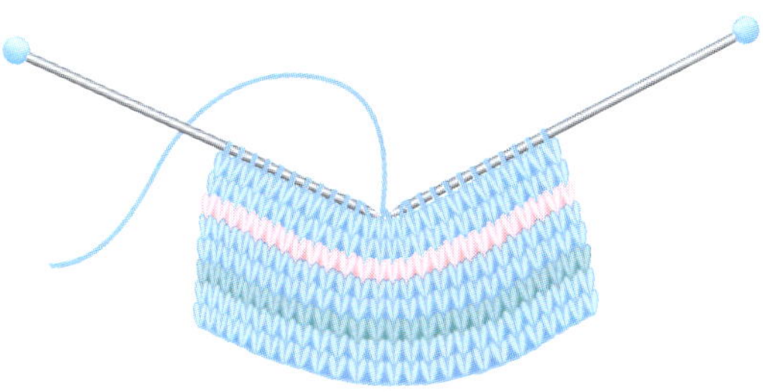

knit

kn | i | ck | er | s

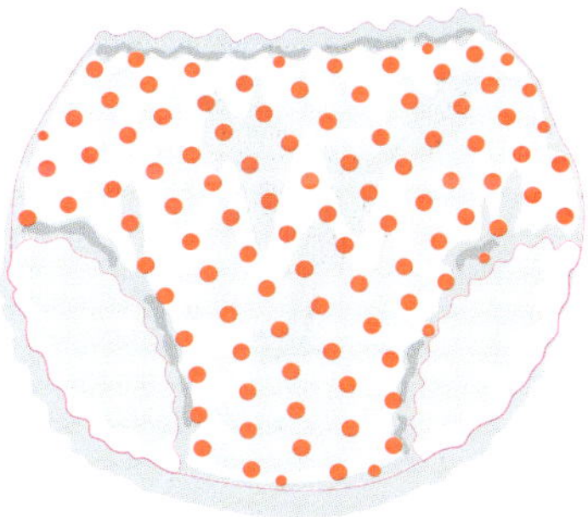

knickers

Make the words

Make the words with **kn** that says n.
Read the rhyme.

This is the [ ] igh | t that lost his [ ] i | f | e.

He [ ] o | ck | s on the door

And [ ] ee | l | s on the floor.

When wr says r

wr | e | n

wren

wr | i | t | e

write

Make the words

Make the words with **wr** that says r.

Read the rhyme.

I [ ] o t e a word

It wasn't long.

But the [ ] i t i ng was [ ] o ng.

What a [ ] e ck of a word

I [ ] o t e.

When mb says m

c	o	mb

comb

b	o	mb

bomb

Make the words

Make the words with **mb** that says m.

Write the words. Read the words.

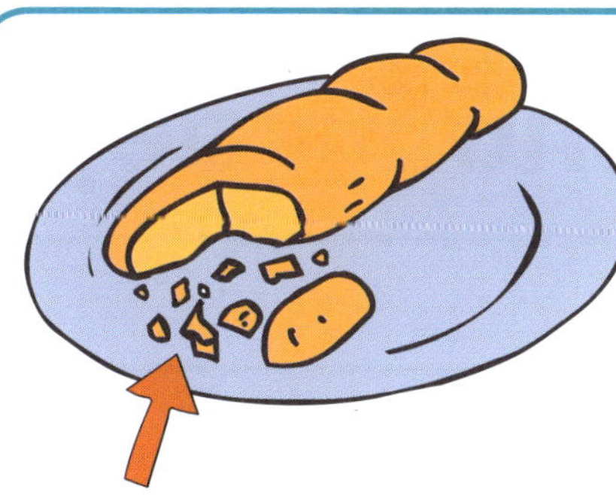

What have I learned?

Note to teachers

Present the exercises one at a time. Explain that they will show the learner what he/she has learned. Use encouraging words such as 'See if you can read the words in this exercises by yourself'. Tell the learner that there will be some words he/she might never have heard before but that they can be sounded using what the learner knows about letters and sounds.

Explain to the learner what to do. For correct solutions, use words such as 'Well done', 'You did well.' If incorrect, praise the learner for having a try: 'It doesn't matter if you get things wrong. That's how we know what you need to practise.'

Read the words and names.

Exercise 1

tray	loud
today	Roy
snout	deploy

Exercise 2

dirt	reach
birch	law
beak	pawn

Exercise 3

new	Tuesday
drew	toe
fuel	goes

Exercise 4

haul	race
tied	slate
turkey	hike

Read the words.

Exercise 5

poke	tiny
jawbone	limb
tune	acorn

Exercise 6

monkey	dead
fern	fly
slow	worth

Exercise 7

calm	spare
heard	cheer
dare	floor

Exercise 8

doorway	pour
core	naughty
before	always

Exercise 9

call	while
install	photo
when	optician

Exercise 10

match	badge
itch	photo
fetch	picture

What have I learned?

What have I learned?

Read the words.

Exercise 11

kneel	action
chef	badger
obey	echo

Exercise 12

vision	magic
facial	gnome
gym	adventure

Exercise 13

wreck	playtime
listen	fairground
fracture	inside

Exercise 14

sound	borrow
auburn	phone
brief	these